VIKING
VIDEO MARKETING

Chapter 1:

Intro to Video Marketing

Why Video Marketing?

Video is arguably the most powerful, trending mode of marketing and communication today. It drives more engagement than any other form of content out there. It boosts conversions like few other things can. It is seen as a must-have for any business both because it is indicative of their ability to keep up with the times and also because it's what audiences want. As humans in the information age become increasingly less interested in reading textual content (thanks, public schools) and more interested in quick and easy gratification and passive entertainment, video is increasingly replacing (or at least displacing) most other forms of content marketing. Here are some stats that may shed some light on this powerful trend.

64% of consumers are more likely to buy a product after viewing a video. 50% of executives look for more information after seeing a video about a product or service. 87% of online marketers are using video content. One-third of all online activity involves watching video content. Video ads make up over 35% of total online ad spend and enjoyment of video ads increase purchase intent by 97% and brand association by 139%.

In addition to the stats and trends above, video carries with it severa other benefits. Firstly, consumption is more likely with video content. People are becoming less and less likely today to read through textual content in its entirety. This applies to everything from eBooks and reports, to blog posts and articles. Consumption of video requires less effort on the part of your audience and more information can be digested in a shorter amount of time.

Secondly, video has the potential to appeal to and accommodate more learning styles. Text is just text. Audio is just audio. But video can be just about anything. Depending on the style of video presentation, a video can be mostly or partly textual. In those cases, a video, assuming it is narrated, can appeal to visual, textual, and auditory learners all at the same time. No other mode of communication has this type of versatility.

Finally, although this may come as a shock, video content can actually be easier to produce. This depends, of course, on a number of factors. If a video is in either "talking head" or screen recording format, it can actually be quicker to produce and convey than writing an article or blog post (this assumes that the videos do not require large amounts of editing or post-production). Even explainer-style videos can be easier and quicker to produce than textual content, provided that you or your video guru have become particularly skilled at throwing explainer videos together. It's also worth noting that with video content, there is no need for proofreading, which can take up a lot of production time by itself.

Chapter 2:

Organic Video Marketing

Although there is much to be said about sales videos and video ads (we'll get those later), it seems there is nothing more powerful for brand awareness, right now, than a competent organic video marketing strategy. There are many places to implement such a strategy, but it makes sense to start with the big one.

YouTube

With over a billion users, YouTube's user base encompasses almost one third of all internet users. YouTube gets over 30 million visitors per day and, on average, those users watch 3.25 billion hours of video each month. YouTube's dual status as a social media platform on one hand, and one of the world's largest search engines on the other makes it, perhaps, the most formidable weapon in a content marketer's arsenal.

The ways in which YouTube can be used in a marketing strategy are plentiful. First, there is the "vlog" or video blog model. In this model, a person or business would simply post video content to YouTube on a regular basis in the same way that one might post to their blog regularly. These video posts would typically be organic and non-salesy in nature. These could consist of any form of video content including interviews, product reviews, how-to videos, and so on. As with any other form of content marketing, an organic video marketing strategy would need to include a plan for consistent content creation.

The Others

Although there are other video sharing sites out there, there are none that come close to YouTube in scale. The two that come closest, however, would be Vimeo and DailyMotion. DailyMotion is the most similar to YouTube in that it's user base is mostly ordinary people sharing and consuming video content. Although DailyMotion's user base is only a fraction of the size of YouTube's, it is often praised for having higher quality content. Vimeo, on the other hand, has a slightly different user base than YouTube or DailyMotion. Although a certain percentage of Vimeo's user base are ordinary people sharing and consuming interesting or entertaining video content, a sizable portion of their user base is made up of video enthusiasts. Vimeo has carved out a niche as being the home of "exclusive", high quality video professionals and enthusiasts. Artists, videographers (both by trade and by hobby), and amateur film producers tend to flock towards Vimeo due to its smaller, tight-knit, exclusive community and its emphasis on high quality video content. From a content marketing perspective, DailyMotion and Vimeo certainly can serve the same purpose as YouTube. However, both sites place greater restrictions on things like video size and length. That, combined with the fact that the potential audience is smaller, usually drives most organic video marketers to simply opt for YouTube instead.

Facebook

One place that has recently seen a sudden rise in organic video marketing, is Facebook. Facebook, has been expanding its video sharing engine and encouraging the use thereof increasingly in the last year or so. Today, Facebook users can upload and post videos to their timelines, pages, and groups. Facebook videos are displayed cleverly in a way that makes them auto-play with no audio while users scroll past them which catches the eye and results in more viewers stopping to view the videos. This has led to Facebook video posts having very high levels of engagement.

In addition to easily uploading videos, Facebook has recently introduced live video broadcasting. Users are now able to broadcast themselves live at the click of a button which, like any other post, results in their contacts being notified of their live broadcast and the subsequent sudden appearance of a sizeable live audience. With all of these recent developments, Facebook has now become an effective and sought-after venue for organic video marketing.

Organic video marketing has clearly come a long way and is a crucial part of any online marketing strategy today. However, equal progress has been made in the realm of paid video advertisements and that is what we'll be covering next.

Chapter 3:
Video Ads

The foundation of a good brand presence and content strategy certainly is organic video content marketing. However, when it comes to acquiring leads or customers, encouraging specific actions, or "jump starting" your organic content, video ads can be an indispensable tool. We'll discuss a few different types below.

YouTube Ads

YouTube ads, when they first came on the scene a few years ago, were a very exciting development. Today, their charm still has not worn off. From a marketer's perspective, YouTube ads are a dream come true. With YouTube video ads, you can make your video play in front of just about anyone at the very beginning of the YouTube video they are trying to watch. All you need is your own video to use as a video ad. Any video hosted on YouTube will do. As if that wasn't cool enough, you only pay the already low prices per view if a person watches beyond the 30 second mark of your ad. This means if a person clicks the "skip ad" (and the majority of people will) button any time prior to 30 seconds, you pay nothing. This means that you are basically spreading brand awareness for free in the case of the "skippers", and paying a very small amount of money in the case of the people who view more of your ad.

There are numerous ways to target audiences with your YouTube video ads. Some of the more common ones include keyword searches, interests, and basic demographics such as age, gender, location and so on. However, the real magic in YouTube advertising, is the ability to target specific videos or channels to place your ads in front of. This means you have the ability to place your ads in front of relevant or even competing product videos. Finally, because YouTube ads are part of AdWords, you have the ability to utilize google tracking/remarketing audiences. In other words, you can place an ad for your product in front of a person who has been to your sales page but chose not to purchase your product.

Google Display Network Ads

In addition to video ads showing on YouTube itself, Google AdWords also allows you to display your video ads all over the web via its display network. This means, if you want, your video ads could be showing in the sidebar of Forbes. The targeting principles for these ads are more or less the same: you can target based on keyword searches, age, gender, location, and various other criteria. Furthermore, by utilizing retargeting pixels, you can use these display network video ads to follow your site visitors around the web with your videos.

Facebook Video Ads

Facebook video ads have become increasingly popular recently. All the usual things about Facebook ads in general that make them so attractive, apply to Facebook video ads as well. The ability to target Facebook users based on interests as well as several other very useful Facebook demographics and targeting options, make Facebook video ads an incredibly powerful tool. But beyond targeting, Facebook video ads are even more impressive due to the manner in which they are displayed. Facebook video ads, like Facebook organic content, auto-play, as they appear on people's screens. This makes your ads all the more noticeable and leads to very high engagement rates for Facebook video ads.

Jumpstarting Organic Content

One little known advantage of video ads is the ability to use them to jumpstart your organic content. Putting a piece of video content on YouTube or Facebook for organic purposes is great. But, you don't need to sit and wait for views to slowly trickle in. You can, instead, give your organic content a quick initial boost by using those organic videos as ads. In the case of YouTube, this simply means starting a new YouTube video ad in AdWords, and choosing your organic content video as the ad video. Target an audience relevant to that video as you ordinarily would, and fire up the ad. This can be an effective way of boosting the number of initial views and engagements in a very short amount of time. In the case of Facebook, once your video post has been made, you simply need to choose the boost post option as you would with any other post. Here, you're simply setting a small budget of $5-$20, choosing a target audience and "boosting" the post which simply means making it into an ad temporarily.

Chapter 4:

Video Production

Once you've decided what your video marketing strategy will look like, you'll need to start producing your videos. There are several different styles and formats of videos requiring varying levels of expertise, software, and equipment. We'll discuss a few of them below.

Talking Head

The talking head format involves this involves sitting or standing in front a camera to deliver your message. This is obviously the style most people are likely to shy away from but they can be an extremely powerful way to deliver a message and create brand trust and familiarity. Any HD camera or even a high-quality webcam or smartphone camera will do. Ensure an excellent microphone is used (ideally a lapel mic) and make sure your lighting is optimal.

Screen Recording

This simply involves using any screen capture software to record your screen while you demonstrate or explain a process or review a product or whatever it is your doing for your video. Because the clarity of text is super important for these videos, you'll want to ensure you are recording at an optimal resolution. Also, since the only thing your audience will notice about you is your voice, you'll need to ensure you use a high-quality microphone.

Slide Presentation

A slide presentation video is exactly what it sounds like. You're simply delivering a narrated presentation using your preferred slideshow software. When you're done you'll simply export it as a video file or, alternatively, you can use a screen recording software and record yourself giving the presentation. As with the screen recording style, your audience will only have your voice to judge you by, so ensure your audio quality is as high as possible.

Explainer Video

Explainer videos have grown in popularity in recent years. These are fun, easy-to-follow, and usually quick-paced animated videos explaining a product, process, or concept. These can be put together relatively easily with any explainer video software like Powtoon.

Advanced Videos

If you have the tools and skills necessary, you might create an advanced high production-value video. These are robust, professional-quality videos that can mix narration, talking head, or interview-format videos with high quality stock footage and a catchy soundtrack. These require a little bit of editing skill and are usually outsourced to a professional.

Tools

For talking head videos, any HD camera will do, including your smartphone or even a high-quality webcam. You'll want to ensure you either memorize your script or use a teleprompter of some sort, such as the teleprompter apps that can be found for tablets on the app store. An inexpensive set of studio lights wouldn't be a bad investment either. Don't bother with greenscreen or even white screen backdrops. These are overrated and very few people ever get them right even after wasting a ton of time trying to get them set up. Your office or living room are perfectly fine backdrops. If you absolutely must use a backdrop, opt for the simpler white screen. Please don't waste your time trying to key in cool backgrounds on a greenscreen. For video and audio editing and post-production, you'll want a good software suite like Adobe Premiere or Adobe Audition.

For screen recordings, a free screen capture software like Jing might be sufficient, but paid tools like Camtasia, Snagit, and Screencast-o-Matic tend to have higher video quality. For slide presentations, use any presentation software like PowerPoint and simply import your narration file or narrate in realtime while recording the presentation. Explainer videos can be made very easily via online tools like Powtoon and GoAnimate. If you choose to use a narration, simply upload your audio file and ensure your animation synchs to the narration while creating it. Finally, for advanced videos like the ones we discussed above, you'll want access to stock footage sites like VideoHive or VideoBlocks and will likely be spending a lot of time editing in Adobe Premiere.

The most important take away from this guide is that video marketing, although it may seem daunting to some, is actually within the grasp of everyone. Not only is it very POSSIBLE, but its arguably a critical part of business today if you're looking to keep up with your competition and grow your brand online. However, none of what you learned in this guide will count for anything, if you don't take action and start applying it today. So, make a resolution to implement the battle plan below right away.

Battle Plan

Step 1: Develop a video content plan based on the information you've learned in this guide including choosing which venues or platforms you'll be focusing on.

Step 2: Acquire the necessary tools and begin producing your videos in whichever manner and style you feel comfortable with.

Step 3: Utilize paid video advertising to gains leads sales, or simply to jumpstart engagement with your organic video content.

Step 4: Continue developing content on a regular basis and stay consistent with your video marketing plan.

www.ingramcontent.com/pod-product-compliance
Lightning Source LLC
Chambersburg PA
CBHW040931210326
41597CB00030B/5267